DYSFUNCTION
is Not
LOVE

The Simple Way to Freedom

RUTH ROBINSON

Dysfunction is Not Love
The Simple Way to Freedom
by Ruth Robinson

Printed in the United States of America

ISBN 9781498401197

www.xulonpress.com

DEDICATION:

ᘒᙏᙚᓭ

ALL GOD'S CREATION

SPECIAL THANKS TO:
MY CHILDREN, GRANDCHILDREN

I AM CLOTHED WITH POWER FROM ON HIGH

⌒☙

I AM FREE! I AM LOVED! I AM NEVER ABANDONED! I AM SECURE!

I AM WHOEVER AND WHATEVER I CAN VISUALIZE. OH NO! HERE WE GO WITH MORE OF THESE REPEATS FOR FANTASY FAILURES! THIS IS NOT WHAT: I AM, IS ABOUT. AS YOU READ ON, YOU THE READER WILL FIND PEACE WITHIN YOUR HEART AS MINE TOUCHES YOURS WITH "TRUTH."

I AM, IS CENTERED ON BIBLICIAL TRUTHS OF ALL DENOMINATIONS: PAST, PRESENT, AND FUTURE. I MUST SEE THE INNOCENT CHILD IN MYSELF FIRST AND THEN IN ALL OTHERS.

THIS IS THE ONLY WAY I CAN PRAISE THE SPIRITUAL CHILDREN WITHIN BY AFFIRMING ENCOURAGEMENT (LOVE=CHARITY). THE, I AM, WITHIN ME, MUST NEVER DEPEND UPON OTHERS FOR WHAT I THINK I WANT OR NEED FROM THEM. THIS IS IMPOSSIBLE FOR THEY CANNOT GIVE ME WHAT I NEED. ONLY THE TRUTH ABOUT ME WILL DO THAT AND THEN ALL IS COR-RECTED. WE ALL WEAR BLINDERS WITH WARPED FALSE MINDSETS.

MY GOD SEES THE INNOCENT CHILD IN ME THAT WAS BORN INTO A WORLD OF PEOPLE WHO DID NOT KNOW WHO THEY WERE, BECAUSE OF GENERATIONAL IGNORANCES WITH LOW-SELF ESTEEM BLINDING THEIR MINDS. AS ANSWERS EVOLVE, PEOPLE WILL SOMEDAY BE RAISED TO BE THE ADULTS AND HAVE THE TYPE OF LIFE THEY WERE MEANT TO HAVE. WE ARE AT PRESENT, LIVING IN MORE PREVELANT AWARE-NESS OF SPIRITUAL ENLIGHTMENT ABOUNDING EVERYWHERE ON THE SAME LEVEL OF UNDERSTANDING IN

ALL DIFFERENT FAITHS AND RELIGIONS, WITHIN WALLS OF VAST AND DIFFERENT LIMINTATIONS!

JESUS, ELVOLVED INTO ONE ACCORD, ONE FRAME OF MIND, AND ONE UNDERSTANDING WITH GOD. JESUS SEEN THAT THE HUMAN RACE KNEW NOT WHAT THEY DID AND WAS ABLE TO PRAY FOR OUR FORGIVENESS.

IF I DID NOT LIVE IN MY FULL POTENTIAL, HOW COULD I TEACH MY CHILDREN TO LIVE IN THEIRS? I COULD ONLY TEACH THEM THE "LACK," I SAW IN MYSELF AND MY PAST CHILDHOOD SO AS NOT TO REPEAT IT, AND GIVE THEM MORE OF EVERYTHING I FELT I DID NOT HAVE. EVEN SO, I AM STILL LIMITED BECAUSE OF MY ILLUSIONS DERIVED FROM MY PERCEPTIONS; AS WERE MY PARENTS, MY PEERS, LEADERS, ETC.

ONCE YOU FACE AND ACCEPT THIS TRUTH AND UNDERSTAND THE REALITY OF IT, YOU ARE SET FREE. NOW, YOU CAN DEVELOP YOUR TRUE, FULFILLED, AND REMARKABLE "I AM SELF!"

⊕⊕⊕

The Lord God is good and reigns forever in your heart as well as in heaven and on earth by all the signs of life you see everywhere. Never cease to recognize all of God's beauty, love, and statements of future goals to be manifested right here on this earth in your lifestyle now.

TABLE OF CONTENTS

ᏙᏙᏙ

Chapter 1: Knowledge Wisdom
Authority 13

Chapter 2: Your New Heredity 25

Chapter 3: Revealing Affirmations 29

Chapter 4: Be Happy Daily 33

Chapter 5: Cruize Ship of Life 43

Chapter 6: High Self-Esteem 49

Chapter 7: Manifestating Heaven
on Earth. 55

Chapter 8: One-Minded Manna 61

Chapter 9: Love 67

Chapter 10: Refuge 77

Chapter 11: Functional 89

Chapter 12: Buried Treasure 97

About the Author 109

Chapter 1

KNOWLEDGE WISDOM AUTHORITY

ᘒ

Knowledge: Understanding the consequences of your ACTIONS and CHOICES in life.

Wisdom: Knowing every "side-effect" in detailed purposes AND VALUES IN COMPARISON TO GOD'S WILL.

Authority: Study and learn your true heredity. You are the SEED of Abraham and our Lord and Savior Jesus Christ!

The family lineage consists of families leaving legacies of obedience to God through Christ Jesus to be passed on from generation to generation until Jesus returns.

As *I reflect back on my past, my appreciation of God's grace and goodwill astonishes me beyond words! God has graciously seen fit to release my soul from prisons of past ignorance's that {EVIL} used then, even in my newborn, childhood* days, as dysfunctional patterns of physical, mental, and spiritual abuse, although *seeming to be normal.*

Evil deceives with ignorance. Ignorance cannot build-up. Ignorance destroys. Ignorance is innocence. Wisdom must present the holy, happy, glorious, and victorious eternal salvation message that can and would have and will bring priceless understanding that produces knowledge.

POWER FROM ON HIGH

The Spirit of God rests upon you and he is glorified on your part, because you "bear" the name of Christ! (1Peter 4:14)

You must give all your anxieties, worries, and physical pain to the mighty hand of God. You must be immovable, determined, and established in your faith! (1 Peter 5:7-10)

No matter what evil seizes upon you, you will not be devoured. God will finish by making you what you should be and grounding you securely. Other Christians worldwide share this same calling. God's grace gives you all blessing and favor, because he has called you to his glory in Christ Jesus.

(GEN. 1:27) SO, GOD CREATED HUMAN BEINGS, MAKING THEM TO BE LIKE HIMSELF, AND BLESSED THEM AND GAVE THEM POWER OVER ALL THE CREATION AND TO HAVE MANY CHILDREN AND LIVE OVER THE EARTH AND BRING IT UNDER "THEIR CONTROL."

(GEN. 3:22) THEN, THE LORD GOD SAID, "NOW, THESE HUMAN BEINGS HAVE BECOME LIKE ONE OF US AND HAVE KNOWLEDGE OF WHAT IS GOOD AND WHAT IS BAD.

We are clothed with power from on high through the resurrection of JESUS CHRIST. When you correct your thoughts with, God said, "Let us create____ (your name) ___ in our own image; abundant joy must abound richly in your heart. You are the created image of GOD, JESUS, and THE HOLY SPIRIT!

We have the authority to calm any irrational thoughts, which brings emotional decay. Thoughts are subject to your command. They cannot intrude where they do not belong. You are the captain of your ship of thoughts. God gave you that freewill. You must give the command, speak the word of God, and they have to flee!

You must know firmly in your heart, that anyone who disowns Jesus, the only Master, brings destruction upon himself or herself AUTOMATICALLY!

(II Peter 2: 4, 5) (Amp.) For God did not (even) spare angels that sinned, but cast them into hell, delivering them to be kept there in pits of gloom till the judgment and their doom?

(Gen.19: 24) And he condemned to ruin and extinction the cities of Sodom and Gomorrah, reducing them to ashes (and thus) set them forth as an example to those who would be ungodly. Find as many other examples in the bible of your choice as to the consequences for disowning Jesus as the son of God.

You now know that once you have been born again, you are not only free from guilt and sin, but free to find out the magnificent creator that you are. Meditate three times a day on this one TRUTH.

(ROMANS 10:9)

Because "if" you acknowledge and confess with your lips that JESUS IS LORD and in your heart believe (adhere to, trust in, and rely on the truth) that God raised Him from the dead, **you will be saved. (AMP. BIBLE)**

The only way to correct your thoughts, increase in strength, and be in God's grace is to study and learn God's word; or you may be carried away by wicked and lawless people. You must consciously choose to continue growing in understanding, recognition, and knowledge of our Lord and Savior, Jesus Christ the Messiah!

READ: PSALM 146, ONCE A MONTH

How can I choose anything of value, while the process of revealing wisdom, is chosen in Ignorance? That's like Russian roulette! You must have knowledge and understanding, especially in the Spirit realm.

Once you know every side-effect of your choices in detailed steps, power is given to you freely by the wisdom of the Holy Spirit, if your free will is of obedience to God. Manifestations arrive with every destiny thought, followed by action.

My habitual thinking and imagery, molds, fashions, and creates my destiny. Jesus said, "For as a man thinketh in his heart, so is he." The desire to pray must be manifested in your daily living. How? As a person thinks, feels, and believes, so is the condition of his mind, body, and circumstances. Infinite riches are all around you when you open your mental eyes and behold the treasure-house of infinity within you. Whatever you want, you can draw forth by the covenant of God. It is your right to discover that covenant world of light, love, and beauty, as well as power. Though invisible, the forces are mighty and capable of breaking all strong-holds in your life, finding the solutions to every problem.

The Bible is simple, clear, and beautiful. Whosoever shall say unto this mountain, be thou removed and be thou cast into the sea, and shall not doubt in his heart; but shall believe that those things which he says shall come to pass; he will have whatsoever he saith. (Mark 11:23) Remember the key principals: DOUBT AND UNFORGIVENESS. Trust, have confidence, let go and leave all unforgiveness toward others or God will neither forgive your shortcomings and failings. (Mark 11:23-33)

Belief creates the law of your mind. All your experiences, events, conditions, and acts in life create your bondages or freedom by the reactive force of your thoughts. This explains why 2 siblings have different lives. What you allow yourself to think becomes who you are. You are enabling the results of your life by what you think. No, this is not just Positive Thinking. Please continue to further your freedom from strongholds by reading on. We can do nothing without Jesus Christ. He is the teacher and we are the students.

(Philippians 4:9) Practice what you have learned and received and heard and seen in me, and model your way of living on it, and the God of peace (of untroubled, undisturbed well-being) will be with you. (Amplified Bible) Your prayers are answered according to the universal laws of action and reaction. Thought is ACTION! We must busy our minds with the concepts of harmony, health, peace, and goodwill. You are the gardener of your mind. You are planting seeds (thoughts) all day long. Based on your habitual thinking, you are either in control or controlled. As you sow in your thoughts, so shall you reap in your body, life, and environment?

"I INHERITED THE BLOOD-LINE OF JESUS CHRIST BY MY FATHER, GOD! MY ADOPTIVE GENES ARE THAT OF GOD & JESUS. I AM THEIR OFFSPRING BY MY SALVATION. THE HOLY SPIRIT ENABLES AND EMPOWERS ME WITH MY RESUR-RECTED AUTHORITY AND POWER BY AND THROUGH THE NAME OF MY LORD AND SAVIOR, JESUS!

Some of the blessings you will reap by turning to God are listed below. Make a sheet of other blessings you have reaped in addition to these. Take as needed with repeated readings and additions.

1. Freedom from bondages that you were unaware of.
2. Intimacy, trust, joy, and Holy Communion with God's power!
3. Sharing your success with others for the glory of God.

4. Fulfilling joy and ecstasy between you and God.
5. A much closer walk with Jesus.
6. Creating your true image that fulfills your purpose in God.
7. Living your life to its fullest creativity within you.
8. Knowing that you "are" walking in the Spirit.
9. Never being full of worries that produce more strongholds.
10. Prosperity in wholeness in every detailed area of your life: (You will bear good fruit. Your understanding will be manifested now in your lifestyle. You will learn to wear the whole armor of God. You will be strong in Christ with a Christ like attitude. Your body temple will be glorified by glorifying God and Jesus will fellowship with you. You will have a joyful union with the Lord, as well as the power Christ gives you by his indwelling Holy Spirit!)

You must now pray daily that from this moment on, you'll never ignore coming to God to be fed instead of sin's selfish desires. You belong to Christ Jesus and can put to death all of your desires by the Spirit who lives within you and is there with you now and everywhere you are and will take control of your life. This is one of the most important aspects to your spiritual faith increasing with power.

Give all your thoughts and thought-producing words to the Lord's Plate of Righteousness and your pallet will be satisfied. Worship with words of praise and thanksgiving within your heart. Praise God he does not reject your prayers or keep back his constant love for you. Thank God for making you and most of all, for allowing you to belong to him. For his love is eternal and you must magnify and worship God with joyful praise.

Confession is critical for it replaces longings for strongholds with longing for God's word and to praise and uplift him, only. You must continuously thank the Lord for "rescuing you" from all of your stronghold cravings and pray for Him to replace all of your unwise desires with guidance from the Holy Spirit. You will be guided into satisfaction. Obedience brings security while being freed from bondages!

The Lord, our God will never cease to fill your cup, your plate, and your mind with wisdom and insight, as well as increase in your hunger for Him. Prosperity in every area of your life follows as you renew your mind and pray; with a heart pure of devotional holiness and obedience unto God first and only. Let the Lord's holiness engulf all of your heart, soul, and mind. Then you will crave desire, need, ask, seek, knock, and you will find.

The Holy Spirit enlightens you if your willingness of heart is sincere for the Lord to tear down, cast away, and put death all "False Gods" that _YOU_ have allowed to lead you out of your freedom by the blood of Jesus!

Once you choose the spiritual righteousness of God, you will know how to rebuke and speak power that devours evil. Satan will be bound by who you are in Christ Jesus. You will know what it means when you pray to seek only after God's ways, follow Jesus' path and crucify your fleshly desires daily, while taking up your cross.

Self-control is a fruit of the Spirit. Self-control is your ability to choose your thoughts. Your thoughts determine your journey in all areas of your life. Understanding the consequences is the 1st step in knowledge. Get this truth into the deepest part of your mind. Ask the Holy Spirit to correct your thoughts when you feel the flesh activating feelings of anger, jealousy, and all those opposite to the fruit of the Spirit. He will gladly do it! That is his business. For rapid advancement in self-control: Key into Chapter 2's following lessons.

Chapter 2

YOUR NEW HEREDITY

თოთუ

Write down the Holy Spirit's perception verses yours.

Ask the Holy Spirit to see for you before entering the situations.

Learn more about the Holy Spirit and his nature.

Listen for the Holy Spirit's guidance in your thought.

You inherited the adoptive Blood-line of Jesus Christ by our Father God! Our adoptive genes are that of God and Jesus. We are their offspring. The Holy Spirit enables and empowers us with the resurrected authority and power by and through the name of our Lord and Savior, Jesus!

Father God loves us with the only rich overflowing intimate love that ever has been and ever will be! He already instilled his love for you by giving his son, his Unity; to you. The Holy Spirit is your birthright, your birthmark, and your heritage!

Just as earthly parents conceive their child, God and Jesus conceived you by the Holy Spirit. The Holy Spirit now lives in your Spirit and Soul because you have Jesus as your Lord and Savior, according to Romans 10:9: guiding your Spirit by God's grace and heredity.

Jesus is your confession upon which your knee does bow. Now your family tree is complete. The Old and New Testaments record our lineage! You are under the blood of Jesus and his bloodline is yours. (On earth as it is in heaven)

We will see our ancestors, our family in heaven. But, we can also read about their life while they were in their earthly bodies, in their day and time, from the Bible. This is our earthly and heavenly family too. Our brothers and sisters in Christ surround us and are many. Let your mind conceive this truth and dwell upon it, as well.

WE ARE ONE THROUGH THE RESURRECTED BLOOD OF GOD.

WE ARE ONE THROUGH THE LOVE OF GOD.

WE ARE ONE THROUGH THE WORD OF GOD.

WE ARE ONE THROUGH THE LAMB OF GOD.

Chapter 3

REVEALING AFFIRMATIONS

ᏫᎿᎥᎽᎿᏌᎧ

THE THINGS YOU AVOID DOING ARE EASIER AND MORE REWARDING THAN ALL THE ONES YOU DON'T AVOID DOING

+ + + REVEALING TRUTH AFFIRMATIONS

1. I AM CLOTHED WITH POWER FROM ON HIGH.
2. BECAUSE OF GOD'S PROMISE, I AM CLOTHED WITH POWER FROM ON HIGH, THROUGH CHRIST JESUS, AS MY LORD AND SAVIOR.
3. BECAUSE OF WHO I AM IN JESUS, GOD HAS CLOTHED ME WITH POWER FROM HEAVEN.

4. I AM CLOTHED IN AND WEAR THE POWER OF JESUS, AS A BELIEVER OF HIS GLORIFIED RESURRECTION.

5. I AM CLOTHED IN GOD'S GLORY AND POWER, BECAUSE OF HIS PROMISED SON, JESUS.

6. GOD PROMISED ME THE POWER OF THE HOLY SPIRIT, BY BELIEVING IN HIS RESURRECTED SON, JESUS CHRIST.

7. I AM WEARING THE PROMISE OF GOD, AS A JESUS BELIEVER.

8. GOD KEPT HIS PROMISE TO ME AND GAVE ME POWER FROM ON HIGH, THROUGH JESUS.

9. THE HOLY SPIRIT IS MY OWN PER-SONAL PROMISE OF POWER FROM ON HIGH, THROUGH JESUS.

10. GOD GAVE ME MY OWN PERSONAL POWERFUL HOLY SPIRIT, BY HIS PROMISED SON.

11. MY POWER FROM ON HIGH COMES FROM GOD'S PROMISE TO ME, THROUGH JESUS'S RESURRECTION.

12. I HAVE PROMISED POWER FROM GOD, BECAUSE I AM A BELIEVER IN JESUS.

(JUST BY LEARNING ONE AFFIRMATION "WEEKLY AND IDENTIFING YOURSELF TO IT, YOUR CHRIST EMPOWERMENT WILL MANIFEST DIVINE AUTHORITY OVER ADDICTIONS THAT RULE YOUR LIFE. ESPECIALLY, THOSE THAT SATAN HAS USED TO ROB, STEAL, AND KILL!

ONLY YOU CAN PUT THIS FORCE INTO ACTION

AFFIRMATION: 2

I AM CLOTHED WITH POWER FROM ON HIGH; THROUGH CHRIST JESUS, AS MY LORD AND SAVIOR, BECAUSE OF GOD'S PROMISE.

The Holy Spirit's perception has enlightened me into a deeper and more efficient way toward wisdom in my life. As I continue to ask the Holy Spirit for understanding in the way of personal issues in my life, that I know I am blinded too, I am allowed to see the Light. (The truth that brings good news to my feelings sensory) Then when I no longer feel the pain of hurt, which is the starting point to depression,

I am free to go about my other business with a clear head.

Chapter 4

BE HAPPY DAILY

I have and am being used by God and have been blinded to that fact because of trying so hard to see things through my own understanding, even when I have prayed for guidance, I still was in the way. I still was leaning on my own understanding and not realizing it. How? Because I had not "grown" to a higher level, even though I thought I had! The more you trust God to make good from everything you consider bad in your life, whether big or small, you are brought into the incredible pathway of understanding. Understanding leads you to knowledge. Knowledge guides you to wisdom.

Look up the meanings to: knowledge
understanding   wisdom

Do you want to feel happy? Do you want to smile a lot? Do you want to feel loved? What about joyful? Do you want to have emotions of peace and contentment, as well as hope? Life can be positive all the time, no matter what is going on. Life can be exciting and brand new.

The Holy Spirit becomes more than just a guide. He becomes a comforter, as well as your companion in everything you do. He never leaves you. He is always waiting for you to ask for direction. He gives direction in matters of the heart, mind, body, spirit, and soul. He never controls unless you invite him too. God gave the Holy Spirit to us through the request of Jesus. The Holy Spirit is part of Jesus and God. The Holy Spirit wants you to know who is with you. The Holy Spirit will comfort you if asked!

I just recently was blessed with the revelation that the Holy Spirit wants me to call him by his name. Not Jesus, Lord, or God, but Holy Spirit. Although part of the trinity, the Holy Spirit becomes a personal comforter when called by his name. When this revelation came to me, I was confronted with the question from him, "Don't you want to be known by your name? "When asked what you do, don't you want to be known by your name relating to your job duty?"

Well, the Holy Spirit feels the same. That's how he's able to communicate to us as we grow from level to level. Just as he communicated with Jesus, the Holy Spirit waits for you.

The Holy Spirit also told me that he wanted a simple "Thank-you," after he gave me direction in what I called upon him to do. Again, he said, "Don't you want a simple thank-you after doing what was asked of you by someone?

Whenever you are trying so hard to figure anything out, that's the time to quit. Consider it a warning signal. You must stop and ask the Holy Spirit to correct your perception and then expectantly wait quietly for it!

Don't know what to wear? Ask the Holy Spirit. He's the best clothes designer, decorator, coordinator, and your own personal expert on everything! Jesus loved and loves us so much, that our minds cannot fully comprehend the wisdom of the Holy Spirit. Jesus could only send us greatness beyond what we could dream of. Anything from God is divine intelligence. Jesus told us that we could do nothing without him!

Read John 20:21, 22, and 23. We have been sent forth by Jesus, just as Father God sent Jesus forth. God will never disappoint you. God needs to use you. God loves everyone more than you love yourself or anyone else. Remember whatever your flesh thinks is the right way to do things, is wrong. Only God's way is wise. God can do anything! We must be addicted to Jesus. We cannot afford to miss one step God has planned for us, in order to reach the souls waiting on our arrival along their path. To know God's will for me:

1. I MUST DAILY STUDY THE SCRIPTURES
2. OBTAIN THE HELP OF GODLY FRIENDS
3. BE GUIDED BY THE HOLY SPIRIT

We must get only in order to give. God blesses us so we can give to others. (2Cor. 9:6-10) We reap everything we sow. We can be richly blessed in all areas of our life and spirit life. The weapons we fight with have divine power to demolish all strongholds! We must take captive every thought to make it obedient to Jesus Christ while being confident that we belong to Jesus and boast freely about the authority the Lord has given us. (2nd Cor. 10:17,18) For it is when the Lord thinks well of me, I am approved! Not when "I" think well of myself. (2nd Cor. 10:3-8,

Mt. 13:14,15, Isaiah 6:9:10, Mk. 4:12, Luke 8:10, John 12:40) My thoughts are my God. My God reigns through my thoughts. Thy Kingdom come, thy will be done. You must take captive all of your thoughts. Your thoughts only hurt or heal you. Once I choose my thoughts, the God Image Power of my freewill is manifested. I crucify Jesus and me with my bad thoughts and the world's thoughts. Bad thoughts are not only those of evil and lust but any that do not line up with the will of God. What thoughts I think, not only comes back to my reality of what I will think of myself; but they also give dominion authority to rule over all of my relationships. Low self-esteem develops as well as bad behavior patterns, which open the doors to strongholds. You have power over every one of your numerous thoughts by your knowledge of who you are in Christ Jesus.

Doubtingly questioning the promise of God will not give you strength or empowerment of faith to move any mountain, large or small, in your life. Wavering about with unbelief or distrust in God's word weakens your faith. Weaken faith produces weak hope. Weak hope manifests confusion. Doors now are opening for fleshly desires and Satan's attacks. Your whole armor is not being worn. We must be fully satisfied and assured that God is able and mighty to keep his word and his promises! (Romans 5:1-5)

Justified means declared acquitted, righteous, and given a right standing with God. We have the peace of reconciliation to hold onto and enjoy. Now, you must continuously rejoice, praise, and exult in your hope of living eternal enjoyment with God. Think upon these things and your heart and emotions will be full of joy, as well as faith, hope, and charity.

Right now, you can be full of JOY. You can triumph and praise God in your troubles and rejoice in your sufferings. How? Why? Because you know God's word says these things produces patient and unswerving endurance. You'll have the fortitude that develops maturity, approved faith and tried integrity. All wavering about will vanish because you will produce within yourself the empowerment of God's love that has been poured out in your heart by the Holy Spirit. You will truly know God's generous love as a benefactor of the anointed one, the Messiah, Jesus Christ.

Our job here on earth, in this fleshly body, is to receive the Gift of God, which is the Holy Spirit. The Baptism of the Holy Spirit gives us power and the ability to witness to others about Jesus' resurrection! <u>Read Acts, chapter 1.</u>

After Jesus' resurrection, he showed himself to his chosen apostles for 40 days and spoke with them about the kingdom of God. While Jesus was eating with them, he commanded that they wait in Jerusalem for the gift God had promised: **The Baptism of the Holy Spirit.** The chosen apostles obeyed Jesus' instructions and joined together in constant prayer along with Mary, the mother of Jesus and Jesus' brothers and with the women in the upper room. The number of believers was 120.

Remember: Joining of constant prayer with other chosen believers and Obedience to the word of God: Jesus.

How do we have power?

How do we have the ability to witness to others about Jesus' resurrection?

(Yes, my friend, only by the Baptism of the Holy Spirit.)

The Holy Spirit is our power and our witness of God's covenant with us through his resurrected son. We cannot be chosen people for the Holy Spirit to manifest God's glory through without accepting, receiving, and rejoicing in the baptism of the Holy Spirit. Why would Jesus have sent us the Comforter after he ascended to Heaven if the Holy Spirit's only job is to comfort us?

What about the Spiritual Gifts? Are they for the Holy Spirit to keep? The only way God is to be glorified through you and me and everyone else is by our Spiritual Gifts. Those Spiritual Gifts direct us to the right course of action within which to perform our talents unto God for his manifestation in the flesh here on earth. Jesus knew this as he used his spiritual gifts unto the glory of God for healings, teachings, and so much more that the Bible couldn't contain them all.

(John 4:24) God is a Spirit (a spiritual Being) and those who worship Him must worship Him in spirit and in truth (reality). Amplified Bible.

We must restore the divine image of God in us: the Holy Spirit! Who is God to you? Can you compare God to anyone or thing? Do you have head knowledge or knee knowledge? Do you really feel with all of your emotions that God is truly good, as well as gracious? Would you like to meet God? DO NOT FORGET, YOU ARE THE DAUGHTER AND SON OF THE ALMIGHTY GOD.

The knowledge of God is in the face of Jesus. God is Love. What was the message of Jesus all about? How do we receive God's Love? By taking down the walls of protection from past hurts. Stop holding anger and bitterness in your life that God allowed what we think he should have stopped. Disappointments reveal hidden idols. Three barriers to God with idolatries that need freed are:

Forgiving God　　　Hurts　　　　Rejection

When you have the ability to let people in, you let God in! Walls of protection keep you from feeling hurts. Difficulty to pray, unanswered prayers, confusion, and anger hides within you. We must then, immediately, confess all or any of these emotions to God in order to be rid of them. That is when the Holy Spirit is freed to cleanse and reveal God's love to you and so the beginning of your one on one relationship with God becomes a delight! Ask the Lord to show you what he sees when he looks at you**! We close off God's Love and our growth by what we believe about ourselves.** Self-rejection and low self-esteem keeps you punishing yourself and always making you just a servant, never a son. When asked, the Holy Spirit will reveal those lies and what they are all about. By <u>believing</u> you deserve God's love, the love of God will get inside of you! God calls his children, Beloved. Did you know that God rejoices, delights, and is happy over you? You are his masterpiece. Remember holding your newborn baby or holding a newborn baby? What did you feel as your emotions ruled over your thoughts? Our feelings are great to us and can bring health and life to our being just from a loving look, touch, or thought. That is a very small example of God's love for us that we are able to feel for others in this human and spiritual form. God's love for us is so much greater than words can say or than we can image. We must continuously work on conforming our thoughts to being lovable, knowing it, and acting like it. Your greatest sin is your unwillingness to let God love you!

Chapter 5

CRUIZE SHIP OF LIFE

~∞~

AFFIRMATION: 3

BECAUSE OF WHO I AM IN JESUS, GOD HAS CLOTHED ME WITH POWER FROM HEAVEN

(Acts 3:16)   Faith in and by the *name of Jesus Christ* brings Healing!

(Acts 3:1-29)   Repentance brings: erasing of your sins and refreshing from the presence of the Lord!

(Acts 4:12)   The only way to Salvation is in and through the *name of Jesus.*

(Acts 5:32)   To receive the Holy Spirit, your heart must be right with God.

(Acts 5:39)   How to know God's will? You will not be able to stop, overthrow, or destroy it.

(Acts 5:41)   Rejoice and continue to proclaim the Christ when you are shamed for the namesake of Jesus. <u>(Read all of 1Cor., chapters 12-14 for more understanding.)</u>

In the scripture references above, you would be well advised to read the entire book of Acts, while taking each verse and asking yourself as many questions as you can think of about each verse. You may think of when, how, symbolic, literal, etc, and all that opens your mind to the guidance of the Holy Spirit. Trust in the Lord and ask the Holy Spirit to tell and show you *what you need to learn.*

This also is true with the "fruits" of the Spirit. Do you know in your heart and mind what they are? I suggest that you learn, for your benefits as a child of God are also found there! The fruits of the Spirit are: love, joy, peace, patience, kindness, goodness, faithfulness, gentleness, and self-control. Whatever you need, at whatever time and whatever the situation, ask the Holy

Spirit for it! *IT IS AS SIMPLE AS THAT.* You must do some research into these fruits. Most people memorize and quote the fruit of the Spirit in church and at weddings. That's usually as far as it goes. We have the right (privilege) to ask, seek, knock, and find. Ask the Holy Spirit for whatever fruit you need for the occasion. That is your right as a child of the Living God through the blood of Jesus! The Holy Spirit is in charge of our guidance as well as comfort. Jesus sent Him to lead us to wisdom concerning the gospel and the power of the Holy Spirit in us. Once you accept this truth, you know you are not alone. You never need to feel alone again. Joy will swell up in your heart to the point of overflowing when you think upon these spiritual things from above. You will want to read, study, and memorize your bible because it is the word of God. All the answers are there. One of my favorite affirmations given to me by the Holy Spirit after Bible Study on the morning of Jan. 22, 1999 is:

I AM ON GOD'S CRUIZE SHIP OF LIFE! THE HOLY SPIRIT IS MY COMPASS! GOD IS MY CAPTAIN! JESUS IS MY NAVIGATOR! MY DESTINATION === HEAVEN!

(Psalm 91) Because I love God, he protects me. Because I know my Lord and Savior, Jesus Christ, I acknowledge Him. When I call to God, he answers me. When I am in trouble, God will be with me. God rescue's me. God honors me. God rewards me with long life, both earthly and eternal.

How to have skillful and Godly wisdom in order to have a successful life:

1. You must have discernment in truth and error (God and Satan): (Positive Thinking (Holy Spirit) versus (Negative Thinking (Human Flesh) in the affairs of your everyday life and your personal mindset of spiritual/non-spiritual beliefs! Whatever You acknowledge as your heredity and traits, is who you will become.
2. Persist, force yourself to listen with all your attention and train of thoughts directed to skillful and Godly wisdom until you learn it and use it.
3. Place yourself wherever you must be in order to demand your heart and mind to be one with (unto) understanding.
4. Daily plead for insight and lift your voice for more understanding!

5. Reverence for God is the only path that leads to abundant life, security now and eternal.
6. *Without Jesus as your Lord and Savior, you are alone. Alone and Doomed!*

Faith through and by Jesus will give us (you, me) perfect soundness of body before everyone. (Acts 3:16).

LORD, MY DAILY PRAYER IS TO BE FILLED WITH AND CONTROLLED BY THE HOLY SPIRIT.

In the name of Jesus and through the power and authority of Jesus Christ of Nazareth, I am whole! Remember the "Name," and what that name possesses. (Acts 4:10)

(Proverbs 3:26) The Lord keeps me safe from "all" hidden dangers and I am confident in this because my confidence is firm and strong in the fact that I belong to God through the blood of Jesus Christ, the resurrected Savior.

How can you be used as Peter was? (Acts 4: 8) You must be filled with and controlled by: The Holy Spirit! You must trust in, rely on, and believe in the fact that Jesus is the Christ! Then when you say: In <u>the name</u> and <u>through the power</u> and <u>authority</u> of the one and only crucified and resurrected Jesus Christ of Nazareth, whom God raised from the dead**; it is in Jesus and by the means of Jesus that all people can be well and in sound body**. There is salvation only through Jesus.

Chapter 6

HIGH SELF-ESTEEM

ᏮᎳᎥᎥᎥᏬ

How to pray for full freedom over all bondages: (Acts 4: 24-31)

YOUR MIND:

must be united with and to God's mind. You must know who God is, God's position in your life, and your rights as God's son or daughter. Being of one heart and soul with God. Loving to communicate with Father God. Loving to run into God's arms.

Knowing that you are never first without putting God first even though you think you are number 1 and put yourself or someone else or thing first above God. You are deceiving yourself. You are blind and leading yourself around without a Seeing Eye dog. Your (evil) fleshy desires want to fill your heart with lies so you will attempt to deceive the Holy Spirit.

You must ask the Lord for forgiveness when your lust, desire to be "boss," and your tantrum fits, lead you, because it's what your flesh (Satan's lies) wants. Ask the Lord to tear down, cast away, and lead you by seeking only after God's ways, following Jesus' path, and crucifying your fleshly desires daily, while taking up your cross. Then your eyes will be opened and your blindness will be gone. You will be healed, whole, and in God's will and all that is ahead are anticipation, excitement, faith, and joy. Love has conquered all!

PRAYER: THANK YOU, LORD JESUS FOR SPIRITUAL INSIGHT INTO THESE TRUTHS ABOUT ME, WHO I AM, AS A HUMAN BEING AND THE KNOWLEDGE I HAVE OF GOOD AND EVIL GIVEN TO ME BY MY CREATION IN THE IMAGE OF GOD, UNITED IN THE TRINITY GODHEAD. I PRAISE YOU LORD, FOR THE KNOWLEDGE TO CHOOSE CHOICES PRESENTED BEFORE ME DAILY. KNOWLEDGE THAT MY FREEWILL CHOOSES, YEARNS FOR, AND IS HUNGRY AND THIRSTY FOR YOU, PRECIOUS LORD. NOTHING ELSE OR NO-ONE ELSE WILL EVER SATISFY THAT NEED. **MY FREEWILL**

CRYS FOR GOD. MY FREEWILL KNOWS THAT WITHOUT LETTING JESUS LEAD ME THAT I AM BLIND AND DESOLATE, FOOLED, TOSSED ABOUT, AND WASTEING MY HUMAN TIME AND LIFE ON THIS EARTH. SATAN LAUGHS AT ME WHEN I DEPEND UPON OTHER THINGS OR ME FOR COMFORT. IN JESUS NAME, I GIVE MY FREEWILL TO GOD'S HOLY SPIRIT WITHIN ME TO LEAD ME! (Now I know in my heart and soul that evil dysfunction cannot use me, fool, or destroy me! IN THE NAME OF JESUS, I AM SAFE IN THE ARMS OF GOD AND THE BATTLE OF MY MIND IS BOUND BY THE AUTHORITY IN AND THROUGH THE POWER OF THE NAME OF JESUS IN MY LIFE. I TAKE AUTHORITY BECAUSE OF WHO I AM AS A CHILD OF GOD AND GIVE ALL CONTROL OF MY FREEWILL TO THE HOLY SPIRIT WITHIN ME! I WILL CONTINUOUSLY OFFER UP THANKSGIVING AND PRAISE UNTO YOUR GLORY LORD FOR SETTING ME FREE FROM PRISONS OF BONDANGES. I know I must daily pray these affirmations as I do the Lord's Prayer.

AMEN

(Mt. 13:8-23) To "reap abundantly" here on earth, you must be those who hear the Word and holds it within their heart and understands it. You will then indeed have knowledge of what the kingdom of heaven means. (Mt. 13: 24-52) <u>Verses 37-43</u>. He answered; he who sows the good seed is the Son of Man. The field is the world, and good seed means the children of the kingdom; the darnel is the children of the evil one, and the enemy who sowed it is the devil. The harvest is the close and consummation of the age, and the reapers are angels. Just as the darnel (weeds resembling wheat) is gathered and burned with fire, so it will be at the close of the age. The Son of Man will send forth His angels, and they will gather out of His kingdom all causes of offense (persons by whom others are drawn into error or sin) and all who do iniquity and act wickedly, and will cast them into the furnace of fire; there will be weeping and wailing and grinding of teeth. Then will the righteous (those who are upright and in right standing with God) shine forth like the sun in the kingdom of their Father. Let him who has ears (to hear) be listening, and let him consider and perceive and understand by hearing. (Dan. 12:3) (Amplified Bible)

If you have to impress anyone by your words, actions, or outer possessions, you don't know who you are in Christ Jesus! You don't feel important, loved, powerful, or great! Even after you've achieved your false sense of security, you still feel a need for more false respect from others. The cycle continues while leading you around in circles. You still lack inner joy and loving, freedom of true self-esteem. That's why nothing satisfies, nothing works, and emptiness returns only to be never fulfilled. More things can fix this emptiness, more relationships, more drugs, and more time-consuming projects, or maybe a new addiction, maybe, maybe, maybe???

Chapter 7

MANIFESTATING HEAVEN ON EARTH

ⲟⲙⲙⲟ

(2 Corinthians 10: 3-6) (NIV)
FOR THOUGH WE LIVE IN THE WORLD,
WE DO NOT WAGE WAR AS THE WORLD
DOES. The weapons we fight with are not
the weapons of the world. ON THE CON-
TARY, THEY HAVE DIVINE POWER TO
DEMOLISH STRONGHOLDS. We demolish
arguments and every pretension that sets itself up
against the knowledge of God, and we take captive
every thought to make it obedient to Christ. And
we will be ready to punish every act of disobedience
once your obedience is complete.

(Ephesians 6: 10-18) (NIV) *FINALLY, BE*
STRONG IN THE LORD AND IN HIS
MIGHTY POWER. PUT ON THE FULL
ARMOR OF GOD SO THAT YOU CAN

*TAKE YOUR STAND AGAINST THE DEV-
IL'S SCHEMES. FOR OUR STRUGGLE IS
NOT AGAINST FLESH AND BLOOD, BUT
AGAINST THE RULERS, AGAINST THE
AUTHORITIES, AGAINST THE POWERS OF
THIS DARK WORLD AND AGAINST THE
SPIRITUAL FORCES OF EVIL IN THE HEAV-
ENLY REALMS. THEREFORE PUT ON THE
FULL ARMOR OF GOD, SO THAT WHEN
THE DAY OF EVIL COMES, YOU MAY BE
ABLE TO STAND YOUR GROUND, AND
AFTER YOU HAVE DONE EVERYTHING,
STAND. STAND FIRM THEN, WITH THE
BELT OF TRUTH BUCKLED AROUND
YOUR WAIST, WITH THE BREASTPLATE
OF RIGHTEOUSNESS IN PLACE, AND
WITH YOUR FEET FITTED WITH THE
READINESS THAT COMES FROM THE
GOSPEL OF PEACE. IN ADDITION TO ALL
THIS, TAKE UP THE SHIELD OF FAITH,
WITH WHICH YOU CAN EXTINGUISH
ALL THE FLAMING ARROWS OF THE EVIL
ONE. TAKE THE HELMET OF SALVATION
AND THE SWORD OF THE SPIRIT, WHICH
IS THE WORD OF GOD. AND PRAY IN
THE SPIRIT ON ALL OCCASIONS WITH
ALL KINDS OF PRAYERS AND REQUESTS.*

WITH THIS MIND, BE ALERT AND ALWAYS KEEP ON PRAYING FOR ALL THE SAINTS.

Compare these verses to the Lord's Prayer. This is how to have your daily bread (blessings from God). This is how to be delivered from evil and the Evil One!

You can speak Bible verses as much as you want or as prayers, and still be speaking them in vain. Until you change your thoughts, your words have no God Power. They are empty and idle and produce nothing or negative damage and hurt, as well as confusion. You must replace a bad thought with God's Truth by his word for His Manifestation to come forth! You must use what you say as God's Hearing Aide unto repentance and replacement while catching each ungodly, unrighteous thought by communing with the Holy Spirit for perfection.

Fear is not success. To have a successful life, you must have a success-mind-set in Jesus. We must compare man's meanings of words to that of God's word. According to Webster's dictionary: Delight means: to provide great pleasure, to please highly, to have or take great pleasure in, a high degree of pleasure or satisfaction of mind, joy, rapture, that which gives great pleasure, experiencing delight. <u>Pleasure means:</u> the feelings produced by the enjoyment or expectation of good, delight, agreeable sensations or emotions, gratification or happiness, will or choice. <u>Desire means:</u> to wish or long for, crave, want, ask for or request, to express a wish to obtain, ask for or coveted. <u>Crave means:</u> to beg for urgently, entreat, implore, and solicit, to call for, as a gratification, to require or demand, ask, beseech, hanker eagerly for. The only way to get what I want is to delight myself in the Lord. It isn't until I reach this point in my life to know what I want that fills all the missing links. Life is meant to be full and rewarding. That is why Heaven seems so far away and like a dream. We haven't had our Heaven on Earth touch of reality yet. We can but only by looking in the right places! (John 6: 35) Jesus will satisfy your hunger, when you believe on him, you'll never thirst. Read Psalm 103 until you believe it is for you too now in this day and time. God left us his promises for all generations until Jesus returns. Then, turn back to Psalm 91, read and be ready to rejoice!

God desires for everyone to move away from pain toward pleasure. This is how he designed humans to function. Dwell on the fact that if it's pain to give something or someone up, it must and will bring you pleasure and freedom because freedom is revelation to God's will for us. God's truth only sets us free. Side-effects of God's truth are: FREEDOM, SELF-CONTROL, HEALTH, JOY, HOPE, PEACE, WISDOM, KNOWLEDGE, UNDERSTANDING, GOD'S KINGDOM, AND WILL BEING DONE IN YOUR LIFE ON EARTH AS IT IS IN HEAVEN!

PRAYER AFFIRMATIONS
1. *THE JOY OF THE LORD ALWAYS BRINGS ME ALL OF THE DESIRES OF MY HEART.*
2. *THE DESIRES OF MY HEART MANIFEST AS I DELIGHT IN THE LORD.*
3. *LORD, KEEP ME HUNGERING AND THIRSTING AFTER YOUR RIGHTEOUSNESS SO I MAY REMAIN FULFILLED AND BLESSED.*

You must never forget that God gave you a Spirit of POWER, LOVE, A CALM AND WELL-BALANCED MIND, AND SELF-CONTROL. Strive daily to remind yourself of that truth. God did not create you to be weak, fearful, intimidated, or lonely. Satan(evil, ignorance, dysfunction, lusts, hate, greed, envy, pride, jealousy, lying, murder, and all harmful acts done to each other) works hard at his job but once you know who you are and the powerful stuff you're made out of, he will run (Satan has to flee)! Learn your strength. You are a fighter. It's time to stand up and fight for what is legally yours. If you could receive a notice of eviction from Satan, you would be in a deep state of depression and shame for being so stupid! You would be able to see in print what SATAN has stolen from you all these years. Every hope, dream, relationship, job, sickness, money-losses, and who you are and where you are in your life now is the result of trickery on you, your parents, their parents, and all the other people involved in your life. Satan rules you and the outcome of your life and your children's lives until all awake and takes control of your inheritances. It's time to break free and live the good life waiting on YOU!

Chapter 8

ONE-MINDED MANNA

AFFIRMATION: 4

I AM CLOTHED IN AND WEAR THE POWER OF JESUS, AS A BELIEVER OF HIS GLORIFIED RESURRECTION

When you speak the word of God and tell Satan to go; (Mt. 4:10,11) that you will worship your Lord thy God and serve only him, the Devil will leave and then angels come and minister to you!

You then have the ability to pray: Lord, my God, I am your servant. Listen to my prayer and grant the requests I make to you today. Let my obsession be to have no other gods before you. As King Solomon's Prayer in 1Kings 8:22 speaks spiritual prayer affirmations for God's manifestations, so can yours. When you hold back the rain (my blessings) because I have sinned against you, and then when I repent and face your holiness, humbly praying to you, listen to me; forgive my sins, and teach me to do what is right! Hear me and give me victory. Make my enemies treat me with kindness. Sovereign Lord, may you always look with favor on me, one of your children, as you chose me from all the people, to be your own people; as you told me through your servant Moses, when you brought my ancestors out of Egypt, that blazing furnace. Praise the Lord who has given his people peace. May the Lord our God be with us as he was with our ancestors; may he make us obedient to him, so that we will always live, as he wants us to live. May he always be merciful to his people according to their daily needs? And so all the nations of the world will know that the Lord alone is God and that there is no other! May all his people always be faithful to the Lord our God. Amen

How can we obey the first commandment? We must see Jesus giving his life on the cross for us in our mind's eye and then see ourselves trading places with him as he ascends to heaven. You must take Jesus off the cross and put yourself on the cross, giving up your life for him before you can ever love the Lord God with all your spirit, soul, and human self! It is only then that you will have no other Gods and be able to love your neighbor as yourself. You must not have any shame to confess the Lord Jesus as Savior of your life. The major battlefield is in our mind and fights to disown our holiness. (Gal. 5:16) We can only continue to serve God by saying no, rebuking, and fighting off our human desires as well as Satan's evil attempts to keep us focused on fear and failure.

Every time you lower your standard, you loose parts of your focus, parts of your growth, parts of your blessings, and parts of your true identity. Satan is now leading you down to the path of lies and destruction, leading to death and eternal doom. Be on guard and continuously pray that the Holy Spirit leads every second of your daily life, by correcting your thoughts, through your obedience to obey God's word. You must know God's word. You must read, learn, eat, and sleep God's word for divine intervention into the realm of your thought life, which dominates your responses and destination! Affirm the presence and power of God until the very substance of spirit would appear in consciousness. This is faith established on a rock. The power of the spoken word of faith is a creative idea in God's divine mind. All words are formative but not creative. Spirit words lay hold of Spirit substance and power. God's law of harmony must be injected into the inner man, which then produces Spiritual results. The Spiritual spoken word is boosted with Faith, which has an inner force that rushes forth and produces remarkable transformations in the phenomenal world! Use your buttons of Faith by merely affirming the power of the word of God and your consciousness hearing will quicken as you watch Faith (God) do the work!

As you give your thoughts to the Holy Spirit to correct about yourself and who you are in Christ, you must also choose to correct your thoughts about others with the understanding from the Holy Spirit. Let your perception be that of the Blessed Holy Spirit only. You must learn to be flexible when God is doing a new work (new wine) in your life. You must daily encourage yourself in the Lord. We choose to be a conqueror or not. The Holy Spirit is my assistant as well as my comforter. Our goal is to be in unity with the power, greatness, and gifts as we experience oneness with Jesus.

We must never grumble before the Lord over any area of our lives, but only be thankful for all we have and rejoice in the Lord! That is the only way we will every reach Canaan. When we grumble, we prove lack of trust and faith. Grumbling is evil to the Lord's ears and brings God's anger! God's anger devours! God will answer our earnest prayers of oppression, if we keep crying out to him for deliverance and be obedient to his word. But on the way to deliverance, we must not grumble, complain, question, argue, accuse, and re-direct our path and circumstances. We must tend to our own business. Work out your own salvation with trembling and fear. (Numbers 11:1-34)

Be satisfied, thankful, and joyful with what you have before the Lord. It all came from him anyway! Erase critical from your vocabulary and your mind. Be thankful in all things to and for God. Dwell only upon how you trust in God's ways, God's will, and God's direction in your life. Lean not unto your own understanding, but in all your ways, thank God, and know he's in charge and only good will come and only good can come to you through God. We must continue to be one way, one-minded with the word of God. Idolatry is loving or putting anything above God. Whatever we do, must be done for the honor and glory of God. Look and treat all people with thankfulness. Everyone and everything belongs to God. A thankful heart destroys a critical heart! A thankful heart produces manna! A thankful heart produces power of the tongue, which eliminates strongholds. In Jesus name, a thankful heart produces healings as God's will is being done on earth by the Holy Spirit within us through our Lord and Savior, Jesus, the son of God! <u>Thankful means</u>: a warm and friendly appreciation of kindness or a favor received, benefits, pleasing, agreeable, appreciative, regard highly, to esteem properly, and manifest due increase in value or worth. <u>Honor means</u>: official dignity, high public esteem, credit, fame, moral standards and conduct, high respect manifested, distinction, privilege, purity, worthy, noble, upright, noble, deity<u>. Glory means: </u>fame, to celebrate, praise, honor, thanksgiving expressed in adoration; renowned, magnificence, a state of greatness or happiness, and the blessings of Heaven. To exult with joy. To rejoice. To be boastful! To take pride in! These meanings were taken from Webster's Dictionary.

Chapter 9

LOVE

◁﹏▷

To be Spiritual, we must separate our spirit and soul from the physical nature. We must seek after sacred and ecclesiastical things. Our nature must be a religious nature of morality from the word of God. The seat of divine influence is Jesus Christ working in man. The third person of the trinity is the Spirit of Reform, which is the Holy Spirit. Our preference, our desire should display a deep feeling and pursuit for satisfaction through Jesus. Everything you do, you now recognize and know by understanding that you are doing this for the <u>privilege</u> to show honor to God and give God all the glory for bringing what you <u>need </u>into existence in your life! It is as simple as that. Jesus leads and you follow Jesus. Jesus continuously gave God all the honor and glory by being thankful in every situation. He knew how God's law operated and still operates today, never changing. God cannot lie. God has not taken the ocean back or changed his mind about anything or any aspect of his creation, thus including his laws. I can only receive blessings in anything I think or do when I give my father God all the glory. In order for God to be glorified here on earth, it is up to me! For me to love myself, know who I am, and love my neighbor as myself; I must glorify God in all I do! When I give God all the glory for every part of the person I am and where I am in my life, and what I possess; then can I only be blessed abundantly and overflowing. When I give my Father God his rightful place of Deity, he gives me mine! My cup runs over and spills out upon those who receive the overflow.

How can Jesus shine through us? WHEN WE GLORIFY GOD, WE CAN'T HELP BUT SHOW JESUS! We are then manifesting through our physical senses and body: our flesh, which we are as a daughter/son of God! Our Spirit leads and our flesh follows. We are walking in the Spirit and not fulfilling the lusts of the flesh. **Jesus can touch others through us when we give God all the glory, honor, and praise. This is putting God first and having no other Gods.**

<u>Memorize this prayer affirmation</u>:

WHEN JESUS SHINES THROUGH US (ME), WE (I) ARE (AM) THE LIGHT OF THE WORLD!

As we all know, there are two sides to a coin. Remember to observe and mediate on the other side of the above affirmation. When evil shines through (me) us, (I) we (am) are the darkness of the world! When we glorify Evil, we can't help but show Satan! As you reap, you will sow. Bind that upon your heart and mind like a tattoo! This is irrevocable. This is truth. Accept the truth and you will be free. Free from all strongholds that keep you bound. MY THOUGHTS ARE MY HOLY GROUND! I AM GOD'S PRIDE AND JOY!

The Holy Spirit works in and through you while correcting all the errors in your life daily when obedience to Jesus is the cross you bear. The Holy Spirit shows me within the walls of Divine Love that I am capable of becoming the person I was born to be. I begin to see with my human eyes, "my blessings!" Freedom is released within me covering fear with Divine Love.

Confidence comes naturally as I listen to the Holy Spirit and I know that I am never alone!

The only goals too attain while here on earth, are treasures in heaven. (Mt. 6: 19-22) When your heart is full of Jesus, your <u>entire life</u> will be full beyond satisfaction! *Your conscience tells you what you really trust in if you will observe yourself closely.* Any person, place, or thing can be put in its proper place of order when you really put God first! We must aim and strive daily after God's way of living our lives. Conquering strongholds becomes automatic when God is first. Self-control

is developed along with all the other fruits of the Spirit. <u>God puts you in charge when you put Him in charge!</u>

AFFIRMATION: 5

I AM CLOTHED IN GOD'S GLORY AND POWER, BECAUSE OF HIS PROMISED SON, JESUS

(AMPLIFIED BIBLE)
(MT. 6:21) FOR WHERE YOUR TREASURE IS, THERE WILL YOUR HEART BE ALSO.

1. WHAT IS THE GREATEST GIFT OF ALL?

Yes, "LOVE" is the greatest gift of all. (1Cor-inthians 13: 1-13). We must

Daily: ask, seek, and knock for the gift of LOVE! Implant in our minds what the scrip-tures define as (true affection for God and man) growing out of God's love for and in us.

How do we learn God's kingdom of Love? What is true affection? What about Me?

All we know of love is from past relation-ships. We read about all kinds of love and see love portrayed on television and the movies in various different forms. One can really get lost in this ocean of love. Is there such a thing as lasting love with passion?

Is love and passion separate?

According to the word of God, Jesus teaches all of the principles of passionate love within the Lord's Prayer. You must take the time and effort to seek guidance from the Holy Spirit for correct perception in studying the Lord's Prayer. The Holy Spirit deals with each one of us on an indi-vidual level. What I may be shown by the Holy Spirit will only be what I need to see to bring correction to my understanding as to my past ways of dysfunctional living. Everything will be given to you individually and you will be lead to the meaning of what is given in the Bible. That is what the word of God is for. Everyone who is without Jesus Christ as his or her Lord and Savior is <u>hopelessly dysfunctional</u>. Now that you are saved and have become a child of God, our covenant allows us to <u>completely function</u> through Christ in us!

(Mt. 6: 9-13=THE LORD'S PRAYER) (LK. 11:2-4) Continue reading in Matthew through chapter 7. Also continue studying in Luke through verse 13. Remember that you cannot be fed your daily bread without asking, seeking, and knocking for healing of your dysfunction patterns in thought, speech, and actions. In all your ways, acknowledge the Lord and he will direct your path. Wrong patterns of living are corrected, as you choose to use your God-given wisdom under the supervision of the Holy Spirit, leading to obedience from the word of God and then you are healed at the right time and place. Your next step into the kingdom of God is more healing for more spiritual prosperity within, producing fruit without, so God can receive all the Glory! This is how to know that you are walking in God's will.

To know that you are not alone when you make a decision that you have been praying about and seeking spiritual guidance must give you security. The world can only give you false security. Knowing that God will make good from even bad choices, eliminates worry. Even if we choose wrong, while thinking it was God's Will, and that we heard from him, God will still correct the mess! That then leads us to victory and victory produces joy unspeakable and full of glory! This is why it is crucial to never quit ceasing to pray with prayers, supplications, and thanksgiving. God knows your heart and he listens to your petitions. Satan/EVIL/Human Flesh,   tries to deceive your mind by thoughts such as, "See, you don't hear from God!" And the list goes on and on with nothing but negativity controlling your mindset.

What is Love? <u>Love</u> comes from a pure heart with a clear conscience, which is full of faith. Love is only found in Christ Jesus unto eternal life, all to the honor and glory of God. <u>What is a pure heart?</u> A pure heart is a heart, which obtains mercy because of acting out of ignorance to all of God's ways. A pure heart is one that can give grace accompanied by faith and love in the full knowledge that Jesus gave us acceptance and mercy combined. A pure heart wishes for all men to be saved! A pure heart is not greedy, dishonest, selfish, or critical. Good deeds rule a pure heart. A pure heart seeks only God's will. You can see that both directions can contain a pure heart. The child, uneducated, the mentally ill, and many more categories fall under this form of a pure heart because of God's unconditional love for us.

I have found that God never lets us figure out how the answer to our prayers will come about. When we pray his word and ask that all be done for his glory, God manifests the end results in many different ways because of having everyone involved in the outcome, in the proper places at the right time. We cannot clearly understand what's happening at the time until our answer has been completed and we're now involved in totally different prayers. That's why it is of value to write down every event you can remember in times of manifestations. Those are your miracles that took place! Then, we are able to understand while loving and praising God more intimately as our faith grows and joy abounds within our hearts.

And now, how to have a clear conscience: Psalms 112 says:

Happy is the person who honors the Lord, who takes pleasure in obeying his commands. The good man's children will be powerful in the land; his descendants will be blessed. His family will be wealthy and rich, and he will be prosperous forever. Light shines in the darkness for good men, <u>for those who are merciful, kind, and just.</u> The most important part of wisdom is honoring the Lord. Please finish reading the rest of <u>Psalm 112</u>: "Light shines in the darkness for good men, for those who are merciful, kind, and just. Happy is the person who is generous with his loans, who runs his business honestly. A good person will never fail; he will always be remembered. He is not afraid of receiving bad news; his faith is strong, and he trusts in the Lord. He is not worried or afraid; he is certain to see his enemies defeated. He gives generously to the needy, and his kindness never fails; he will be powerful and respected. The wicked see this and are angry; they glare in hate and disappear; their hopes are gone forever." <u>(Today's English Version Bible of Psalms).</u>

Looking for satisfaction in any area of your life can never, no it cannot be filled by others, things, nor money! Jesus told us how to overcome all strongholds in our life by doing everything in moderation. Whatever vice that is in control of you, can be overcome with self-control. Self-control means basically MODERATION. If you are unable to use your self-control, than this vice (stronghold) must become a simple NO! NO! HOW???????? By replacing it with the Bread of Life, Jesus. Jesus will bring you Total Self-Control when you run to your Prayer Closet, Read your Bible, and Worship God. These pills are your cure! <u>Only you can do them for yourself. Again, this is part of your Freewill. You will be delivered from all evil and temptation will not bother you.</u>

Chapter 10

REFUGE

MT. 6;22 THE EYE IS THE LAMP OF THE BODY. SO IF YOUR EYE IS SOUND YOUR ENTIRE BODY WILL BE FULL OF LIGHT.

MT. 6:23 BUT IF YOUR EYE IS UNSOUND, YOUR WHOLE BODY WILL BE FULL OF DARKNESS. IF THEN, THE VERY LIGHT IN YOU (YOUR CONSCIENCE) IS DARKENED, HOW DENSE IS THAT DARKNESS! (Amplified Bible)

THE ANSWERS BELOW CAN BE OBTAINED EASILY WHEN WE ASK THE HOLY SPIRIT TO LEAD US 24-7 AND WE LET GO AND ENJOY LIVING!

<u>How do we NOT grieve the Holy Spirit? We must lead a life of</u>
1. Behavior that is a credit to the summons of God's service.
2. Living with humility, unselfishness, gentleness, and mildness.
3. Patience, bearing with one another.
4. Making allowances because you love one another!
5. Be eager and strive earnestly to guard and keep the harmony and oneness of and produced by the Spirit in the binding power of peace.

We can find rest in our souls by reading Mt. 11:28. Let Jesus teach you what it means to be gentle and humble in heart. Jesus is our intercessor praying to our Father God on our behalf; pleading all of our requests before God hears our prayers we have prayed to Him. God then grants all the desires of our Heart and informs the Holy Spirit on the directive path to instruct us upon. As we obey God's directions, we never stumble because we are walking by the Spirit!

Because Jesus is our Savior, leader, Brother, Our Deliverer, Our instruction Book of Life, Our Bridegroom, Our Attorney, Our Healer, Our

Passion, Our Lover of Truth, Our Hope, Our Desire, Our Personal Friend, Our Eternal Salvation, Our Example of How We Should Be, and many more titles than any and all words could never describe; God is pleased to give us our heart's desire because it is good. Our heart's desire has to be something from the word of God, because the bottom line is always for God to be glorified when we get what we're asking for. It will keep the flow going for more and more of God's Glory, honor, and praise to be magnified continuously!

In summary, what I ask for is not to take away from God's Glory but will bless God's Glory, not mine! As long as we ask according to the written will of God from his word, then we are being used as human beings visually portraying God while walking in His Divine Will. Mercy and goodness will follow us all the days of our lives. Our relationship with Jesus will flourish; our intimacy with God will manifest divine love. Remember: Do unto God, as you would have him do unto you!

Then our gifts, as well as our growth with God will also be manifested. (Eph. 4:10-32).

(Amplified Bible) Psalm 5: 11, 12++ But let all those who take refuge and put their trust in You rejoice: let them ever sing and shout for joy, because You make a covering over them and defend them; let those also who love Your name be joyful in You and be in high Spirits. +12: For You, Lord, will bless the (uncompromisingly) righteous (him who is upright and in right standing with you); as with a shield You will surround him with goodwill (pleasure and favor). Now, get your Bible out and read Psalm 8: 5, 6. Continue on in Psalm, asking the Holy Spirit for direction, and write or underline "all" the Psalms that touch your emotions with feelings of: strength, honor, pride, success, joy, excitement, pleasure, favor, and many others that you need to feel in order to believe that faith in God's Word includes these emotions. What do you think will happen as you feel God's Truth within your physical body? Yes, Spiritual Understanding, Mental Healing, and Physical Healing will manifest! You can't have one without the other in order to learn of Wisdom and all the riches you can have here now on earth with Father God. Father God created us in his image. Jesus had a physical body while here on earth. Jesus laughed, ate, cried, and was filled with all of physical emotions that we have. Meditate upon what you read before going on to another sentence, paragraph, or chapter. This will allow your physical senses to do the job they were meant to do.

This produces advancement in faith. Advancement in faith produces Psalms 8: 5-9

What is faith? Believing. What is Believing? According to Webster's Dictionary, believing means: to be convinced of the truth, dependability, or existence of something without demonstrable evidence; to have confidence, trust, rely on through faith, and accept on the basis of credibility. We all have tried many things and people to see if they worked or were trustworthy, before our belief in them grew into confidence. Confidence produced faith within us. But before we tried, we had to deal with our thoughts, reasoning intellect, and so on. So, begin here and put Jesus to the test. I guarantee he will pass everyone with exceptional intelligence beyond your wildest dreams!

AFFIRMATION: 6

GOD PROMISED ME THE POWER OF THE HOLY SPIRIT BY BELIEVING IN HIS RESURRECTED SON, JESUS CHRIST

Unfortunately, we human beings use our intelligence and forget to use the only intelligence there is! I'm sure you've heard it said that

God helps those who help themselves. There is no person on earth who can help himself or herself without God. Now, let's use plain and simple common sense. God came to earth in the form of a man, Jesus, to die for our sins and to show us the only true way of life, as we live our time out on earth in human bodies. Jesus sent us the Holy Spirit after he was resurrected, to be our Comforter, Guide, and Counselor. Why would God need us to figure out every aspect of our lives without our Guide leading us? We are to follow our Guide; not our Guide follows us. We have it backwards and are living our lives backwards! We will never go anywhere but backwards. *Only with the Holy Spirit* in his *divine leadership role, we will always go forward!*

We must learn to ask God to change our interpretation of our wants and needs. When we only want what we need, then our wants line up with the word of God for our needs. We now have found satisfaction in our lives. There is no longer the need to keep searching and searching for satisfaction in more things, addictions, etc. Only God can lead you to this Garden of Eden where you truly are to rule in all areas of your life. Self-control, moderation, and wisdom are formed and feed your soul for right choices, God choices.

Without God Choices ruling your life, you and Satan rule your life. Who do you think guides you then? No, not you! You are then in the Devil's Ship of Decievement. You have chosen to help yourself, lead yourself. God is not found there. Satan wants you alone and without God, so that he can persuade you to live his way in all areas of your life. Satan's ways are full of lies, trickery, false hope, false love, which is, really hate, and false pleasure that can never be satisfied. Satan also delights in sickness, disease, mental abuse, physical abuse, pain, depression, self-hate, fear, loneliness, and all the heartaches and deformities of life. *EVEN WHEN YOU THINK YOU'RE HAPPY, BEWARE OF SATAN'S TRAPS.* That's when the Devil has you blinded and unaware of his plan to destroy your life or kill you!

<u>It is impossible to just rule your life yourself.</u>

(Mt. 6:24-7:29) It is a lie that you can serve God and mammon. Anything that you trust in (money, material possessions, job, talents, health, people, or yourself, etc.) and are devoted to, will take the throne of God in your life and all of your blessings! God promises us what we shall receive here on earth if we put all of our trust in Him.

We are NOT to worry and NEVER be anxious about ANY AREA of our lives. This is the bottom line on how to continuously increase our Faith. God knows what we need and He will willingly provide it <u>and much more</u>. We have to learn to believe this with all of our heart and soul. When we earnestly and diligently seek God's Ways of Doing Things, God gives us His Word that He will provide for us! We then cast out all "doubt," that leads to confusion and mistrust, down to the path where Satan lies in wait, to trigger our thoughts and lead us into his guest chamber of Hell on Earth! We have to keep this Holy Respect (Fear of the Lord) implanted in our mind while in these human bodies. Our Spirit is already aware of this. This is our part to accept the things we cannot change and change the things we can! We have to know who we are with or without God. THERE IS NO IN-BETWEEN.

(Mt. 13:44-52) Jesus gives us illustrations with comparisons in story form to alert our minds with His parables. Jesus tells us what the kingdom of heaven is like. We have no excuse not to understand or find it. He compares it to buried treasure that brings great joy, fine and precious pearls, etc. We must read, meditate, and praise God for all the mind-boggling riches He wants to give us right now. Just dwelling on the above scriptures will give us joy unspeakable and full of glory! Jesus begins teaching us in Matthew 5 and ends our lessons at Matthew 7: 29. Open your Bible to these scriptures now and begin a new life-changing journey to your true destiny!

If we can learn to accept Father God as the most wonderful "Daddy" in the whole wide world, we are on our way to "Childlike Faith!" This is why it is crucial to meditate upon the ways of Jesus, God, and the Holy Spirit. As we see all other ADULTS as= CHILDREN, we are released from dysfunctional patterns of thinking. We are then freed from the Strongholds (wrong, bad, evil habits) that keep us from being all that we are supposed to be!

Pick a quiet time for yourself to meditate on how much God loves you. Close your eyes and picture yourself climbing into the arms of your loving Daddy God. Jesus is there too and so is the Holy Spirit. Run and almost jump into his lap while climbing the rest of the way into his soft warm arms that wrap around you. Tell him who hurt you, who made you mad, and all the things that bother you. Feel him love you. Really listen and he will tell you what you need to hear to soothe these feelings coming from these real situations in your life. Ask him anything you want and he will answer you with such unconditional love that your soul will rejoice. Tears will turn to happiness. He may even tell you that all of your feelings are a good thing because they are from your Father God and they were given to you for your own good. If you want, he will teach you all about every one of them and how to use them to really make your life healthy and happy.

(Using food as an addiction (stronghold) will be used now to show how God wants to simplify any problem that keeps us stuck in our traps of hopelessness).

COME EAT WITH ME! Neither TYPE NOR AMOUNT OF FOOD CAN, HAS OR EVER WILL STAISIFY YOU. WHY? You're eating alone. You're eating without me. You can do nothing without me!!! Talk to me; listen to me as you prepare our meal. Set the table for me and then you "join" me (Jesus) as I fellowship with you by our holy communion. I want you to really enjoy food! I want you to love eating. I will *teach you how to really enjoy every bite that you put into our holy body temple. Father god's temple in you will be honored. I'll invite the Holy Spirit to plan your daily events, starting with thanksgiving first, then prayer. Following that comes health and long life to your bones as god's love fills and heals every part of your mind and body with his word, his promises! Anticipation of good, fun, rewarding and new pleasures of this day lie ahead. Gone is any and all anxiety and fear! Take me with you, put me ahead and in charge of you in every thought you have the moment your eyes awaken unto this new day. (Romans 8:8 So then those who are living the life of the flesh (catering to the appetites and impulses of their carnal nature) cannot please or satisfy God, or be acceptable to him. Amplified Bible.*

Chapter 11

FUNCTIONAL

ᏩᎲᎲᎩ

We can never have enough or do enough of anything to keep us content with the life we have here on this earth! The only answer for contentment is to be content in Jesus. No food, no person, no place, or thing can ever fill your cup to the overflowing edge of complete satisfaction, complete fulfillment! It doesn't matter who you are, how old, how rich nor how poor, how thin, fat, pretty, or popular you may be! We must accept this truth before we can ever be free to live a life of victorious living in all we do.

O.K., so what do we do next? How do we really reach this point of truth? You must ask the Lord Jesus what you should do next for the good of God's earthly holy blessed body temple in the condition it's in, now on this day, at this time of your life.

We must choose to listen, tune in, and hear our many different parts of our physical body and senses talking to us and actually trying to tell us what the warning signals of malfunction in our bodies are. We are in charge of these human form bodies for one reason only and that is to magnify the image of God in order to manifest His glory and His kingdom come and His will being done on earth as it is in heaven! That is the bottom line. The more we resist, the more we loose our true identity. We can never find who we are or ourselves. Do some research and you will learn that even all other types of beliefs; have the spirit in charge of the flesh. Even in the medical world, it has been proven that "Stress" is a killer to the physical body. Why? Because God did not create you or me to be without him! God is in charge whether you like it or not because God knows we would destroy everything without His leadership. We are not individual. We are not alone. When you or I fight off the presence of God, then we are killing our physical body, our life, and the lives of others that we are unaware of. We must take this serious. We must cry out to God for wisdom. We must seek to use more than 10% of our brain! We must rejoice in giving God all the glory. That is his rightful place, not ours. We only gain our rightful place when we give God divine authority. We have it so backwards and turned around that we make living hard! Jesus says his way is simple and easy. Do you really want to live the rest of your life only to learn at the end of it, that the joke was played on you by you because of your freewill to be God? Then, all your pain, worry, work, dreams, and fears would have all been in vain, an illusion! To get to the bottom line, your life never really existed! The life God had waiting for you never got to manifest. Who you really are was thrown away and tossed in a corner of time that never mattered!

READ 1 COR. 6:12-20, 1 COR. 10:14, GALA-TIANS 5:22-26, JAMES 4:7, & 17, JOHN 5:30, ROMANS 8:12, 25, and 31.

Now ask Jesus to lead you and keep you on the right course, the right way of doing all things, even how to walk right, stand, sit, sleep, and every physical aspect of God's holy Body Temple that you have been put in charge of here on earth, just as when Jesus, in his human body flesh, was here! This invites holy communication leading to intimacy with your spirit and God. You will once again be walking in the spirit and not fulfilling the desires of the flesh. You will be in unity with God. When our mind is in tune with God, our spirit controls our flesh. When we give our carnal self to God, our mind is given to God automatically. Ask to see everyone and everything through the eyes of Jesus. When all you see is good in others, all you'll see is good in you! So then, all you can get in your life is good! Remember that A THOUGHT=RE-AC-TIONS. Your tongue will become bridled. Your Spirit will lead your soul. Your flesh will be crucified. Your body will respond in rhythm creating wholesome health. Your soul will elim-inate stress and magnify happiness.

Mt. 23:12 How to be exalted: "*Humble yourself.*"
How to self-destruct: "*Exalt yourself.*"

Justice, mercy, and faithfulness must be first in everything you draw on from your soul.

YOUR "MIND" MUST BE HEALED OF ALL ITS DYSFUNCTIONS BEFORE ANY PART OF YOUR LIFE CAN MANIFEST ITS TRUE DESTINY! (That is the meaning of God looking at our heart and not our actions).

Until you are whole within your self-worth by knowing your self-love in Christ, you have made choices in life from a pattern of influences of a house divided. That is why those choices turned out to be the wrong ones. This leaves "confusion" at your doorstep as you proceed to move on to the next page in your chapter of living unfulfilled dreams and desires. So now, being intoxicated with your own intellect, you proceed to make more wrong moves that will eventually put you in checkmate!

Hint #1: God wants you to know how he sees you (not how you see you).

Wisdom, knowledge, and understanding are to be sought after more than riches or any attributes in life. *HEALINGS AND ALL MIRACLES WILL AUTOMATICALLY OCCUR AS A NATURAL SIDE EFFECT WHEN HUMAN BEINGS BECOME FUNCTIONAL!* (JESUS WAS FUNCTIONAL IN HIS HUMAN BODY WHILE HERE ON EARTH). Jesus knew who he was in God. Jesus used his entire mind because it was functional. This allowed his human side to have clear perception of his destiny and all the people and situations involved.

God wants you to know you, like he does: by pleasing yourself with the love of Jesus! It is impossible to please others without knowing the real you. Only then can goodness and mercy follow you, and the side effect will be that you please your neighbors as yourself, because you are in unity with God through Jesus. You will then be "thankful." Being thankful brings praise. Praise brings power. Power brings victory! When you are alone in yourself; (flesh, human nature) you are out of the Garden of Eden!

When you are with God, you then know that before you are able to glorify God, you must allow God to glorify you with his presence, releasing in you, the power to receive his perception on who you are and crucifying the "false" person you have let rule the real you! It is impossible for you and anyone to glorify God when we are "spiritually dysfunctional.

*Before you can love, you have to love you as much as possible compared to God's love for you, which is unconditionally. Only then can you love ANYONE through the eyes of Christ. Thus, God is glorified!

———*MINDSET THOUGHTS*———
GOD SEES THE INNOCENT
CHILD IN ME!

GOD SEES MY FULL POTENTIAL!

GOD WANTS TO ENCOURAGE ME!

GOD IS WAITING TO CORRECT MY
THOUGHTS!

GOD IS WAITING ON ME TO GIVE ME
MY HEART'S DESIRES!

GOD IS ALWAYS WITH ME!

GOD LIVES IN ME!

AFFIRMATION: 7

I AM WEARING THE PROMISE OF GOD, AS A JESUS BELIEVER: (AS A JESUS BELIEVER, I AM WEARING THE PROMISE OF GOD)

Chapter 12

BURIED TREASURE

ᗰᙡᓬ

LUKE 6:38: GIVE AND IT SHALL BE GIVEN UNTO YOU: GOOD MEASURE, PRESSED DOWN, AND SHAKEN TOGETHER, AND RUNNING OVER, SHALL MEN GIVE INTO YOUR BOSOM. FOR WITH THE SAME MEASURE THAT YE METE WITHAL IT SHALL BE MEASURED TO YOU AGAIN.

The word of God is so perfect and easy to understand. The trouble is that we want to do everything our way. And nothing works! With God, all things are possible. In other words, everything works ": With God."

*PLEASE READ CAREFULLY: You have not "Believed" in your Father God's irrevocable law. You have taken away your own return. You did not digest every word and the meaning. (It does not matter if any human being does not give you anything back.) What you think does matter! We must trust God to keep his word. When we do, God's promises will manifest! Give God's ways to others and you will receive the desires of your heart. God knows what he is doing in all of our lives. All we have to do is follow his plan.

WHAT IF GOD DOESN'T GIVE ME THE DESIRES OF MY HEART? THEN <u>YOU</u> **HAVE NOT GIVEN AWAY** <u>YOUR HEART'S DESIRE</u>!

<u>List on paper your true heart's desires:</u>
<u>those things you really need to make you</u>
<u>crazy happy!</u>

You will be replenished every time that you give to others what you need. Of course, I am under the assumption that we are mostly talking about our inner emotional needs. The material will manifest in its proper order.
<u>No amount of material items can feed your</u> <u>soul. Your inner child and adult</u> <u>must be fed</u> <u>with nurturing unconditional Love!</u> You are a storehouse of buried treasure. God treasures you

and the Holy Spirit wants to give you the key to your "treasure house!" Remember, I cannot give you what you need. I can only show you by my ACTIONS what" I need" by GIVING YOU: what I need. No, not by words! Words may be included but my actions and yours speak loudest and show honest feelings. Words cover up and can bring confusion if actions aren't in line with all of our words!

Here are a few examples:

If I need you to be honest with me, I must be honest with you. If I need you to communicate more with me, I must find the time when we both can devote to each other's free time and listen, finds ways of compromise, and both parties leave the communication time satisfied. If I need more passion, I must give more passion. And The list goes on..................................

(Common Sense must help to rule your need to give to others what you need. You have to be considerate of their time, roles, and positions in life. This has nothing to do with being "SELFISH" but with being "GIVING." All too long, we have hidden the lighted candle behind the big bushel. Jesus wants us to learn to let our light shine! Being a child of God, you are full of His Image. Yes, you are full of Love. Clear thinking means clear vision. Your image has been distorted but you have the ability because of who you are in Christ Jesus to wipe the smudge off of your mirror and really see Y O U!)

(Mk. 10:51) And answering him, Jesus said, "What do you want me to do for you? And the blind man said to him, Rabboni, I want to regain my sight! (10:50) Jesus said to him, "go, your faith has made you well! Immediately he regained his sight and began following him on the road. The key word here is want. The blind man wanted his sight so bad that the instant his desires found his need, faith was born to be released into the miracle of vision!

What do you want that is the same as your need? Make a list and journal on paper or in your thoughts, however your mind chooses to bring forth the truth to your attention. I've heard people say that they are now praying for God to send them their needs, not what they want. I even bought into that myself but had to learn that I had to want what I needed before it could manifest and be brought into the light of my sight. I remained blinded by my misunderstanding.

Remember the woman with the issue of blood and all she needed to do was to touch the hem of our Lord's garment and she got what she wanted! She had to do something to get what she wanted. Her pathway was neither easy nor short but she knew what she needed to do, did it, and got her heart's desire!

You must have faith-in-Jesus as your healer. (Mk. 10:51)

The most vital piercing goal one must seek after is Faith. No amount of money, rubies, gold, or silver can give you the intimacy of satisfaction that faith-in-Jesus as your healer can!!!

But how does one obtain such a faith? Ask, seek, and knock so that the doors will be open unto you. But how long? Until you reach your intimacy of satisfaction in the Lord Jesus Christ, God the Father, and the Holy Spirit.

Do I have to become a monk, guru, or saint? I don't know how far your personal intimate journey with the Lord will be; you will know, and God.

Will it be hard? Will it be stressful? Will it be exciting? Will it be painful? Will it be obtainable? When you look into your soul, meditate upon these thoughts, you will understand more than words could tell you. You need words now to guide you into these thoughts of lighting your passion.

You now must become the cultivator of your garden of life that you have left, moment-by-moment, and day-by-day. Remember to ask yourself what can I do to increase my faith? What would I have to do if I had a garden? What would I have to do if I had a business of my own? What would I have to do if I wanted to shape up my body and health? What would I have to do if I wanted to improve any area of my life?

One of the most important words to implant in your mind as the first key is:

"PASSION"
The second is: DETAILS, DETAILS, and DETAILS!

Now the "responsibility" is Yours!!! You now are the captain of your ship. You are your own boss. You do have a part in your life, your true destiny! No, nothing will grow; nothing will multiply abundantly until you put all you have into your true self, your true relationship with

Christ. You cannot count on anyone else to do it for you. If you've been going to church regularly, worshipping daily, or praying 24-7 and your faith is on hold and not producing satisfaction unto you, listen to your passion and ask the Holy Spirit for direction.

We can only do so much and then we have to rest so we can hear the right directions and not be blocked by rapid programs running through our minds. The old saying that "silence is golden," is worth remembering.

Running your life too fast or too slow will not get you anywhere but in repeated circles searching for more empty cycles of unfulfilled wasted time. <u>MODERATION is the key</u> to successful living. Remember, the word of God has all the answers and leads you to the only truth which is full of joyful living! <u>Moderation, Good, and Positive REWARDS, are the actions to use to correct dysfunctional thinking</u>. These actions awaken the powerful enfoldment of spiritual direction as well as faith leading us to the truth of who we are in Christ Jesus.

God loves us so much that he gives us the desires of our heart even though God knows those desires are "not" what we need to be fulfilled in this season of our life. God holds us with surrounding protective hugs and that Divine Love wants us to know that when you "WORRY," you push God aside! You lose all of your Powers and Trust is lost as well. Faith and Hope cannot be found when Trust is Missing-in-Action!

We may cry out with rage, hurt, self-pity, and confusion as to why we try so hard to think this way, act it even if we don't feel it, and still no manifestations of our wants and needs seem to show up. Now what and why even continue this falsehood? Everything seems like crumbs compared to others we know. If we're really honest, we may even really feel deep inside that life is hard, people are selfish, and why bother? Yes, you and I both know that this list could turn into many, many pages of lonliness, isolation, addictions, and warped false mindsets!

Remember, when your feelings are telling your mind what to think, that's the red flag to run as fast as you can mentally to get away from those feelings. How? We grab on to the Olympic mindset of "TRUTH" THOUGHTS! Call them whatever suits your fancy to correct your self-image of who you are in Christ Jesus. My friends, this is all that keeps you SANE! Like anything else, it takes effort and it is daily and many times in one day. You had to learn how to do everything in your mind before physically being successful and this is no different at all ages and stages of your life in every circumstance. It can become easier and almost automatic but no one will and can do it for you. You are the creator of your thoughts when you are enlightened with TRUTH. You have to do the work, develop the skill, seek, knock, and the door again, will be opened. You may read many self-help books, go to different groups, counseling, pastors, and the lists goes on that is available resources for development. We are only at peace when we have our Ignorant Falsehoods replaced with an Intimate Relationship with God! We are centered, happy, healthy, and wise. We replace tears of misery with fulfillment!

AFFIRMATIONS: 8, 9, 10, 11, and 12.

8. GOD KEPT HIS PROMISE TO ME AND GAVE ME POWER FROM ON HIGH, THROUGH JESUS.
9. THE HOLY SPIRIT IS MY OWN PERSONAL PROMISE OF POWER FROM ON HIGH, THROUGH JESUS.

10. GOD GAVE ME MY OWN PER-SONAL POWERFUL HOLY SPIRIT, BY HIS PROMISED SON.

11. MY POWER ON HIGH COMES FROM GOD'S PROMISE TO ME, THROUGH JESUS'S RESURRECT-ION.

12. I HAVE PROMISED POWER FROM GOD, BECAUSE I AM A BELIEVER IN JESUS.

These laws speak to your soul when you digest them into your mind. Truth abounds within your heart bringing hope for the missing link, the hole in the empty secret part of your life, and freedom to have the abundant life meant for you!

ABUNDANT LIFE means happiness, joy, peace, health, anticipation of another wonderful day, love for all mankind, satisfaction with your life and all attributes of yourself, nothing lacking in your heart's desires, full of thanksgiving, being content in your accomplishments, and the list continues to grow!!!!!!!!

You may wish now to make a list of what it would take to make you feel all of the abundant life emotions listed above within your mind's eye of what you need to manifest these attributes. Then review any section of this book and instill these suggestions along with your own. Comparison, will be a helpful guide. You may decide to combine both for better results.

ONCE AGAIN, YOU ARE THE CAPTAIN OF YOUR OWN SHIP: WITH OR WITHOUT GOD.

THE END (OR)

THE BEGINNING

DYSFUNCTION IS NOT LOVE!
DYSFUNCTION KEEPS YOU GOING
BACKWARDS.
***

DYSFUNCTION KEEPS YOU STUCK.
***

DYSFUNCTION KEEPS YOU CONFUSED.
***

DYSFUNCTION KEEPS YOU UNHAPPY.
***

DYSFUNCTION KEEPS YOU LONELY.
***

DYSFUNCTION KEEPS YOU FULL OF
ANGER.*
DYSFUNCTION KEEPS YOU ADDICTED
TO HELL ON EARTH.*
DYSFUNCTION KEEPS YOU IN A PRISON
OF TORMENT.*
DYSFUNCTION FEEDS YOUR LIES.*
DYSFUNCTION ROBS YOU OF YOUR
DREAMS.*
DYSFUNCTION MAKES SURE YOU DIE
FULL OF REGRETS.*
DYSFUNCTION MAKES YOU SETTLE FOR
LESS IN LIFE.*

ABOUT THE AUTHOR

Ruth Robinson was the 13th child from an Appalachian background with insurmountable odds against her. Severe stuttering from the age of 5 was her thorn in the flesh.

As a Williamsburg, Ohio graduate in 1964, she went to college in her mid forties.

Her work background included: Activities Director in Nursing Homes and Rehabilitation Specialist I with Intellectual Disability Clients. Being a single mother for 25 years contributed to her positivity to survive.

Her spirituality as a Christian began at the age of 13. Ruth wrote poetry, did oil paintings, charity work, self-help writings, and motivated everyone she knew.

Her dreams to become a counselor never manifested because of dysfunction.

Ruth Robinson now uses what she shares in this book to see this dream come true, and wishes the same for you…

CPSIA information can be obtained
at www.ICGtesting.com
Printed in the USA
LVHW082152300919
632791LV00018B/869/P

9 781498 401197